RITTENHOUSE SOUNDWORKS

CHANGING SPACES

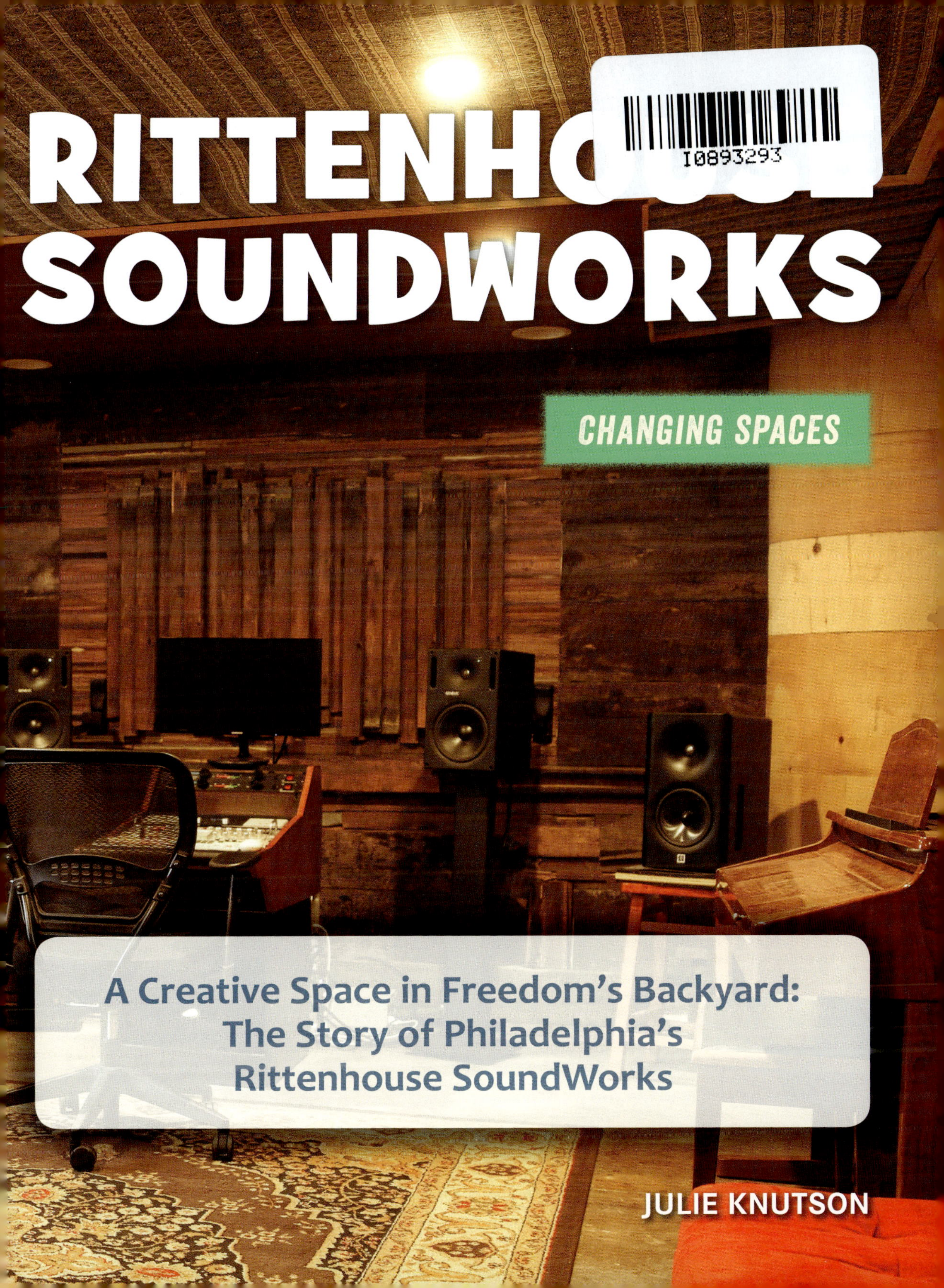

A Creative Space in Freedom's Backyard: The Story of Philadelphia's Rittenhouse SoundWorks

JULIE KNUTSON

CHERRY LAKE PRESS

Published in the United States of America by Cherry Lake Publishing Group
Ann Arbor, Michigan
www.cherrylakepublishing.com

Reading Adviser: Marla Conn, MS, Ed., Literacy specialist, Read-Ability, Inc.
Photo Credits: © Matthew Hamilton, cover, 1, 5, 17, 20, 27, 29; © Przemek Klos/Shutterstock.com, 6; © Jana Shea/Shutterstock.com, 9; © Nina Alizada/Shutterstock.com, 13; © James Kirkikis/Shutterstock.com, 14; © litts/Shutterstock.com, 18; © Nejron Photo/Shutterstock.com, 23; © NBaturo/Shutterstock.com, 24; © castate/Shutterstock.com, 26; © Jill Saul, 28

Cherry Lake Press is an imprint of Cherry Lake Publishing Group.

Library of Congress Cataloging-in-Publication Data
Names: Knutson, Julie, author.
Title: Rittenhouse SoundWorks / by Julie Knutson.
Description: Ann Arbor, Michigan : Cherry Lake Publishing, [2021]. | Series: Changing spaces | Includes index. | Audience: Grades 4-6 | Summary: "Learn more about how Philadelphia's Rittenhouse SoundWorks went from abandoned historic building to vibrant recording studio. Explore the logistics of renovating the building and meet the people who made it happen. The book showcases a range of 21st century skills–from "Flexibility & Adaptation" to "Creativity & Innovation"–and shows how moving away from a tear-down culture towards one of reuse helps tackle a host of critical challenges facing our planet and population. Thought-provoking questions and hands-on activities encourage the development of critical life skills and social emotional growth. Books in this series include table of contents, glossary of key words, index, author biography, sidebars, and infographics"–Provided by publisher.
Identifiers: LCCN 2020006378 (print) | LCCN 2020006379 (ebook) | ISBN 9781534169005 (hardcover) | ISBN 9781534170681 (paperback) | ISBN 9781534172524 (pdf) | ISBN 9781534174368 (ebook)
Subjects: LCSH: Rittenhouse SoundWorks (Firm)–Juvenile literature. | Sound studios–Pennsylvania–Philadelphia–Juvenile literature. | Industrial buildings–Remodeling for other use–Pennsylvania–Philadelphia–Juvenile literature.
Classification: LCC NA6280 .K59 2021 (print) | LCC NA6280 (ebook) | DDC 725/.40974811–dc23
LC record available at https://lccn.loc.gov/2020006378
LC ebook record available at https://lccn.loc.gov/2020006379

Cherry Lake Publishing Group would like to acknowledge the work of the Partnership for 21st Century Learning, a Network of Battelle for Kids. Please visit http://www.battelleforkids.org/networks/p21 for more information.

Printed in the United States of America
Corporate Graphics

With thanks to Jim and Matthew Hamilton

ABOUT THE AUTHOR

Julie Knutson is an author/educator fascinated by the endless ways in which people and communities can transform old spaces for new uses. She lives in Illinois with her husband, son, and extremely energetic border collie.

TABLE OF CONTENTS

Adaptive Reuse—More Than Meets the Eye

ESSENTIAL QUESTION: *How can an old, unused building be adapted to meet the current needs of its community?*

> *"This building was built to be a recording studio, but nobody knew it until we walked in."*
> *— Jim Hamilton*

Just off of one of America's most historic streets, tucked behind a white brick wall sits a barely visible building. Built more than a century ago in Philadelphia's Germantown neighborhood by the car manufacturer Chrysler, it peeks out from behind a windowless

The building's facade gives no hint of the creative work that happens behind its walls.

facade. For decades, it sat hidden and empty. In its crumbling loft, old Christmas decorations collected dust. Water pooled in corners. Worn wooden posts battled with gravity, bending toward its floorboards.

It was a space waiting for someone to enter it and recognize its potential.

Record libraries provide curious musicians and listeners with access to musical offerings from artists working in a range of genres.

Five doors down from this neglected structure lived recording artist Jim Hamilton. He'd catch sight of the odd and out-of-reach building from his backyard while mowing his lawn. What was it? How would you even enter it? Although he lived just steps away, when he finally gained access to it, he still wondered, *Where am I?*

This is the story of how Jim and the historic building at 219 West Rittenhouse Street met. It's also the story of how, after years of touring spaces around the city for a recording studio, he and his family envisioned a new life for this 100-year-old industrial property on their own block. Today, inside its walls, new things are happening. Moments in sound and image are being captured by teams of recording and filmmaking gurus. Community members gather to hear performers from a wide range of musical traditions. Music historians browse its record library, and headphoned teens learn the art and craft of sound engineering at a summer camp.

Seeing the Possible

Jim first toured the studio with his wife, Susan Deutsch. Susan immediately recognized the potential in the space. Jim wasn't so sure. On their second walk-through, they brought a team of builders along. They agreed with Susan: it was a space in which anything was possible.

It's alive again, humming with sounds and energy. It just needed someone to sit in the space and understand its potential for **adaptive reuse**.

CHAPTER 1

A Look at America's Most Historic Neighborhood

Philadelphia's Germantown neighborhood boasts more than 300 years of history. It was the birthplace of American **abolitionism** and the site where the paper for the Declaration of Independence was milled. It was also the location of the first bank of the United States. Germantown is a place that forward-thinking, creative people have long called home. It's a place where change and adaptation are the norm. Known as Freedom's Backyard, it hosted early German colonial settlers who fled religious persecution at home. It was the

Revolutionary War reenactors portray the Battle of Germantown each year.

site of the only battleground within the city of Philadelphia during the American Revolution. Its soils have seen waves of immigration, from both outside the United States and within it. Its streets, buildings, parks, and plots of land brim with centuries of stories.

The Birthplace of American Abolitionism

In 1688, four Germantowners drafted a two-page document **denouncing** slavery, the first of its kind in American history. Guided by the Golden Rule—the belief that you should "do unto others as you would have them do unto you"—the petition was shared at Quaker meetings in the colonies. The document argues that every human possesses basic rights that should not be violated. It also asserts that enslaved people have the right to revolt. Shelved and forgotten until 1844, the document was rediscovered by 19th-century abolitionists and celebrated for showing the long history of their movement to end slavery.

The origins of this settlement at the edge of Philadelphia trace to 1683. William Penn, founder of the Pennsylvania Colony, sold 5,700 acres (2,307 hectares) of land to German settlers unwelcome in Europe because of their religious beliefs. The settlers were diverse, with Quakers, Mennonites, and Dunkards in their ranks. They all had to find a way to live and work together in the new province that was built on the idea of tolerance. Many Quakers—guided by their belief in the "Inner Light" of the divine in all people—were especially vocal supporters of human rights and equality.

The Colonial Era gave way to the Revolutionary Period, and Germantown was a hotbed of the independence movement. In an attempt to recapture Philadelphia from British hands, a major battle was fought on Germantown's streets. This 1777 battle was one of the largest engagements of the war. The neighborhood's Deshler-Morris House served as not only George Washington's home in 1793, but also a decision-making site for the Early Republic.

The Germantown White House

Germantown's Deshler-Morris House is the oldest existing presidential residence in America. George Washington called it home, taking refuge there during the 1793 yellow fever epidemic that swept the then-capital, Philadelphia. The story of that epidemic is retold for young readers in Laurie Halse Anderson's historical novel, Fever 1793.

Germantown Quakers continued their fight against slavery in the 18th and 19th centuries. In the 1850s, the Johnson family operated a secret Underground Railroad "station" from their Germantown Avenue home. Here, they sheltered, fed, and clothed hundreds of enslaved people journeying north in pursuit of freedom. The home also provided a meeting place for abolitionists and is believed to have been visited by Harriet Tubman.

Many people fleeing slavery passed through Philadelphia on their journey north to freedom.

Elferth's Alley in Philadelphia is thought to be the nation's oldest residential neighborhood. Some of the homes are nearly 300 years old.

As the 19th century wore on, European immigrants continued to settle along Germantown's cobblestone streets. In the early 1900s, they were joined by African Americans leaving the **Jim Crow** South in search of better social and economic opportunities as part of the **Great Migration**. The city of Philadelphia's African American population grew from 84,000 in 1910 to 219,000 in 1930. In Germantown, organizations like the YWCA led efforts to build intercultural understanding. This YWCA also pioneered Negro Achievement Week in 1928 to build community and talk back against racism and discrimination. Negro Achievement Week is often seen as laying the foundations for Black History Month.

In a neighborhood this historic, properties that once served a certain purpose are being adaptively reused to serve another. The YWCA building is being redeveloped as apartments and offices. St. Peter's Episcopal Church has been transformed into Philadelphia Waldorf School. People throughout the community are envisioning creative new uses for unused spaces. The folks at Rittenhouse SoundWorks are in good company—and had ample support for transforming 219 Rittenhouse.

"All buildings are alive, especially buildings that are this old. It has a history . . . it's seen more history than any of us."
— Jim Hamilton

CHAPTER 2

Hidden in Plain Sight

For years, the main sounds at 219 West Rittenhouse were squeaking tires and rumbling engines. While the Chrysler facility set back from the street had long been shuttered, the front building operated as the very repair shop where the Hamiltons got their cars fixed. But once Jim became aware of the vacant space at the rear, the sound engineer in him began to think it might provide a good home for new sights and sounds.

On their first visit to the space, Jim had a hard time seeing past the rotting drop ceiling and pegboard walls covered with rusting mechanics' tools. But he gave it a chance. Even today, he notes that it takes time to understand the potential of a living building with

Repairing and repurposing a historic building means you can create almost anything in the space.

this much history. After being assured by a team of contractors that there was nothing that couldn't be fixed, they jumped into transforming the structure for a new purpose. This two-part process involved repairing the building and adapting it for its new **acoustic** function.

A variety of factors, from ceiling height to the material the walls are made of, contribute to optimal sound for recording artists.

First up? Making sure that the building was structurally stable. Sagging posts were tied together with star bolts, which operate like braces, keeping wooden beams in place. Next, walls and drop ceilings were torn out. Behind and underneath them were brick walls and a wooden, A-frame ceiling, which is ideal for sound. The floor, stained with decades of automotive oil and speckled with nails, was refurbished by the Hamiltons and a team of friends and colleagues.

The World's Most Famous Recording Studio

London's Abbey Road Studios is known as the world's most famous recording locale. A combination of three things—its A-frame, wooden ceiling; brick walls; and concrete floor—create a perfect acoustic mix. That same mix is what makes Rittenhouse SoundWorks such an ideal setting for recording artists.

Notice the curved elements on the walls in this room.

The site was then made sound-friendly. Because sound vibrations travel in curved waves, construction crews rounded out 90-degree corners and edges in the building's rooms. Each room became a living math equation in which shapes and forms were selected to enhance sound absorption and diffusion. In the upstairs loft, a massive, open-floor recording area was built out, surrounded by two smaller isolation rooms, where music or sounds would be made, and a sound-mixing chamber, where they would be mixed and recorded. Downstairs, additional recording spaces were added.

The space was divided up to host other creative suites for filmmaking and photography businesses run by Jim's son Matthew. A record library containing thousands of vinyl albums organized by instruments allows musicians the opportunity to study the history and evolution of sound.

In converting the space, the Hamiltons also considered **sustainability** issues. They repurposed old church pews as seating for public events. They removed wood from a former radio, battery, and television manufacturing plant. They used bank glass as door handles and for skylights, and old, curved cable spools from a communications company to create rounded edges in recording rooms. In addition, they generate their own heating and cooling with a biofuels system that creates clean energy out of everything from wood pellets to cherry pits to horse manure.

CHAPTER 3

A Place to Gather and Create

"Basically, recording is the art of taking pictures of air moving. Up here, we take pictures with microphones. Matthew takes pictures of colors where the frequencies are much higher and uses camera lenses to do that. But they're all microphones, capturing energy."

— Jim Hamilton

Today, musicians, artists, and filmmakers from all over the world descend on this multipurpose creative space to capture and share their art. The vast, open floor plan of the upper-level studio allows for huge groups to record together *and* perform in front of live

State-of-the-art recording equipment helps operations like the SoundWorks serve their artists.

The SoundWorks' monthly musical events are a chance for the community to experience different types of music.

audiences. It also allows for public events and gatherings. On the third Sunday of each month, SoundWorks opens it doors to the community for concerts. Equipped with mics and amps, four acts take to the floor, engaging listeners with everything from Brazilian bossa nova to Americana folk sounds.

A Different Type of Salon

While you might think of a salon as a place for getting your hair cut, the word has another older meaning. In 18th-century France, salons were gathering places for people to meet and discuss art, science, philosophy, and literature. Often led by women, they were spaces where the rules of the outside world were rethought and sometimes challenged. The monthly performance gatherings at Rittenhouse SoundWorks—with their emphasis on community conversation and participation—were conceived in this tradition. Jim sometimes refers to these gatherings as a musical salon.

The Greater Philadelphia Cultural Alliance estimates that arts and culture contribute $4.1 billion to the city.

For Jim and the other makers at Rittenhouse SoundWorks, art has the power to transform not just individuals but also entire communities. Germantown is witnessing a **grassroots** revolution in its culture industries, in a city where arts and entertainment constitute the third-largest segment of the economy.

The SoundWorks offers programs for students looking to pursue careers in music or recording.

From car repair shop to vibrant recording studio, Rittenhouse SoundWorks has becoming a beacon in the community.

Jim says, "[Art] doesn't give you a grade or give you a test. Instead it asks who you are as an individual."

In 2015, Jim told *The Chestnut Hill Local*, a local news outlet, "Art is an equalizer. It levels the playing field." This is because art is about ideas and concepts.

Here at Rittenhouse SoundWorks, people meet, create, perform, record, and remix. In adapting and reusing this structure, Germantowners and global performers alike have been given a unique venue in which to capture their own ideas, concepts, and voices.

Extend Your Learning

Jim Hamilton is a drummer who became interested in percussion through an unusual route: tap dancing. Both of his parents were dance teachers, and he eventually discovered the relationship between tap and drums, and tap and jazz music. Today, he performs with music ensembles from around the world. He's quick to point out that musicians are always finding creative ways to produce percussive beats. Often, this involves adaptive reuse of objects ranging from metal pots and pans to cardboard tubes to jingling keys.

Conduct your own experiment in adaptive reuse by making your own percussive instrument out of discarded or unused objects. Create a rainstick by filling cardboard tubes with sand, beads, or rice, and sealing off the ends with parchment paper and rubber bands. Or suspend keys from an old container lid to create a perfectly usable tambourine! The world of sound is yours for reinventing!

Glossary

abolitionism (ab-uh-LISH-uh-niz-uhm) the movement to abolish slavery

acoustic (uh-KOO-stik) relating to sound or hearing

adaptive reuse (uh-DAP-tiv ree-YOOS) reusing a structure for a purpose other than that which it was originally designed to serve

denouncing (dih-NOUNS-ing) saying in public that something is wrong

facade (fuh-SAHD) the front part of a building that faces the street

grassroots (GRAS-roots) a social movement driven by community residents that takes shape from the bottom up

Great Migration (GRAYT mye-GRAY-shuhn) mass migration of African Americans from the rural South to industrial Northern cities

Jim Crow (JIM KROH) laws in the United States that legalized segregation from the late-19th to mid-20th centuries and set different rules for black and white Americans

sustainability (suh-stay-nuh-BIL-ih-tee) done in a way that can be continued and that doesn't use up natural resources

INDEX